KU-570-201

THE
GIANT
BOOK OF
KIDS'
JOKES

THE GIANT BOOK OF KIDS' JOKES

AURA

This edition published in 2014
by Baker & Taylor (UK) Limited,
Bicester, Oxfordshire

Copyright © Arcturus Holdings Limited
26/27 Bickels Yard, 151–153 Bermondsey Street
London SE1 3HA

All rights reserved. No part of this publication may be reproduced,
stored in a retrieval system, or transmitted, in any form or by any
means, electronic, mechanical, photocopying, recording or otherwise,
without prior written permission in accordance with the provisions
of the Copyright Act 1956 (as amended). Any person or persons
who do any unauthorised act in relation to this publication may
be liable to criminal prosecution and civil claims for damages.

Illustrations by Peter Coupe

ISBN: 978-1-78404-325-4
CH004288NT
Supplier 29, Date 0714, Print Run 3473

Printed in China

(Henry Haine)

CONTENTS

What do you call a man who writes joke
books for a living ?

Poor !

What do you call a man with a cable
coming out of his ear ?

Mike !

What do you call a man who does
everything at top speed ?

Max !

What do you call the ghost of a
Star Trek character ?

Doctor Spook !

What do you call a super hero who
looks after books ?

Conan the Librarian !

What do you call an overweight vampire ?

Draculard !

What do you call a woman who works
for a lawyer ?

Sue!

What do you call a man who goes fishing
every weekend ?

Rod !

What do you call a teacher
with earplugs in ?

**Anything you like – he
can't hear you !**

What do you call a polar bear in the desert ?

Lost !

What do you call twin brothers with drums on
their heads ?

Tom Tom !

What do you call a man and woman who show you up in front of your friends ?

Your Parents !

What do you call a man who likes drawing and painting ?

Art !

What do you call a man who does odd jobs and lives just round the corner ?

Andy !

Prisoner - It's not my fault. I was given a name that was bound to lead me into crime !

Judge - What is your name ?

Robin Banks !

What do you call a woman who
hates butter ?

Marge !

What do you call a sumo wrestler
built like a refrigerator ?

Whatever he tells you to !

What's the name of that really
strict teacher ?

Miss Norder - Laura Norder !

What do you call a man who
corrects examination papers ?

Mark !

What do you call a man
with seagulls on his head ?

Cliff !

What do you call a woman who only comes out at Christmas ?

Carol !

What do you call a masked man who lends you money ?

The Loan Avenger !

What do you call a woman who checks punctuation ?

Dot !

I call him Bill - he's always asking me for money !

Did you hear about the man who used to make his living selling refreshments in the intermission at football games ?

His name.......... Alf Time !

What do you call a Scotsman
with his own computer?

Mac!

What do you call a woman
who can juggle bottles
at a brewery?

Beatrix!

What do you call a man who keeps
pet rabbits?

Warren!

What do you call a man who
keeps pet rabbits and writes
epic novels?

Warren Peace!

What do you call a man who
lets puppies sleep in
his jeans?

Very, very stupid!

What do you call the man who stamps the letters at the Post Office ?

Frank !

What do you call a man who works in a perfume shop at Christmas ?

Frank in Scents

What do you call a woman having a meal in a restaurant ?

Anita !

What do you call a Spanish woman having a meal in a restaurant ?

Juanita !

*If you really loved me,
You'd let me call you Jack.
Then you could lift my car and
mend the flat that's at
the back !*

What do you call a snail without a shell ?

A slug !

What do you call the box a toad
keeps his tools in ?

A Toadstool box !

What do you call a man who delivers
Christmas presents to lions and tigers?

Santa Claws!

What do you call a woman with a frog
on her head ?

Lily !

What do you call a woman who was eaten
by her cannibal husband ?

Henrietta !

What is the first surfing
term that vampires learn ?

Hang ten !

What do you call a
baseball player who only
plays at night ?

The Star player !

What was the name of the man who designed
King Arthur's round table ?

Sir Cumference !

What do you call an Ancient Egyptian with no
teeth ?

A Gummy Mummy !

What do you call a woman who sneezes all the
time and likes knock, knock jokes ?

Tish who !

What do you call the pudding that fought at the battle of the Little Big Horn ?

General Custard !

What do you call a parrot when he has dried off after a heavy rainstorm ?

Polly Unsaturated !

What do you call a man with a tissue paper head ?

Russell !

What do you call a man with a wooden head?

Edward !

What do you call a man with an exam paper on his head ?

Mark !

What do you call the place where spooks
go for their weekend ?

A Ghost House !

What do you call a man with legal
documents on his head?

Will !

What do you call a miniature version
of one of the Beatles ?

Small McCartney !

What do you call a pet
that makes a lot of noise ?

A Trumpet !

What do you call a man with very strong
reading glasses ?

Seymore !

What do you call a
woman who
lets you
borrow money ?

G-Lenda !

What do you call a man
made up of
spare body parts ?

Hand Toe Knee !

What do you call a bear that's been caught in
the rain ?

A Drizzly Bear !

What do you call a bee with feathers ?

A Buzzard !

What do you call a man who doesn't sink ?

Bob !

What do you call a bee with his own car ?

A Bee-M-W !

What do you call the illness that martial
arts experts catch ?

Kung Flu !

What do you call the super heroes who got run over ?

Flatman and Ribbon !

What do you call your brother's smelly son ?

My ne-phew !

What do you call an uncontrollable cat ?

Impussible !

What do you call a woman who rescues shipwrecked sailors ?

Mandy Lifeboats !

What do you call a Scottish android ?

Robot the Bruce !

What do you call a woman who works at the zoo ?

Ellie Fant !

What do you call a dessert that hit an iceberg ?

The Pietanic !

What would you call a girl that grew up
in a flowerpot ?

Blossom !

What do you call a glass robot ?

See - Through - P - O !

A garage owner called his first daughter Toyah,
then he called his second daughter Toyah as
well...

She was the spare Toyah !

What do you call a man with a large fiery planet
on his head?

Sunny !

What do you call a girl
who comes out very
early in the morning ?

Dawn !

What do you call a
radio host who plays
records in alphabetical
order ?

An A, B, C, D, J !

What do you call a
man who only eats
casseroles ?

Stu !

What do you call a
Russian gardener ?

Ivanhoe !

School
Screams...

Teacher - You should have been here
at 9 o'clock this morning !

Pupil - Why, did something happen ?

English Teacher - Sally, do you like Kipling ?

Sally - I don't know, Sir, I've never eaten one !

My last school was so rough they didn't have a school photograph - they sent home mugshots instead !

Science Teacher - Gary, do you know what Copper Nitrate is ?

Gary - Yes Sir, it's what they pay policemen on night duty !

History Teacher - Martin, where would I find Hadrian's wall ?

Martin - Wherever Hadrian left it, Sir !

Teacher - Carol, why have you brought a picture of Henry the eighth in with you ?

Carol - You told us to bring a ruler in with us today !

Teacher - name one of Noah's children.

Pupil - Joan of Arc ?

And... for all those who were late this morning because they stayed up to watch the hockey... we're going to make School more like hockey...

you will all stay behind and do extra time tonight as a penalty !

Mathematics Teacher - Kevin, can you tell me the 9 times table please ?

Kevin - You asked me that yesterday, don't tell me you've forgotten it already !

Teacher - You're on English level 4 aren't you, Jon ?

Jon - Yes.

Teacher - Then take this English level 2 book for your father or he's never going to be able to catch up and do your homework properly !

Of course in my day you only had the one choice for school food...................

............Like it or lump it !

★

Where do Martians go to train to be teachers ?

Mooniversity !

I think my teacher is in love
with me...

How do you work that out ?

...she puts red kisses all over my homework !

★

What's the best snake to help you with your arithmetic ?

An adder !

I would have done my homework, but.....

I didn't have any pocket money left, and my sister always demands cash in advance.....

My dad was working late, and he has all the brains in the family.....

My pen ran out and I spent all night looking for an inkwell.....

What fruit does a history teacher like best ?

Dates !

Please Miss, is it true that the French only ever eat one egg for breakfast ?

What makes you ask that ?

Because yesterday you said that in France, one egg is un oeuf !

Did you hear about the teacher who had to wear sunglasses in the classroom?

He had extremely bright pupils!

Anxious parent - What do you think my son will be when he has finished all his exams?

Teacher - Retired!

How many teachers does it take to work the photocopier?

Who cares, as long as it keeps them out of the classroom!

Principal - You boy, stop running around like that! Don't you know who I am?

Pupil - There's a man here who doesn't even know who he is!

Why do swimming teachers like elephants ?

Because they never forget their trunks !

*We've got a new drama teacher -
she's a real class act !*

Principal - That's Hodgkiss, the school bully.

Visitor - How dreadful, can't you do anything
to stop him ?

**Principal - Certainly not, or I'd never get the
teachers back to the classrooms after lunch
break !**

Why did the stressed teacher
keep bending the cane ?

He needed a break !

What should you do if
your teacher rolls her
eyes at you ?

Pick them up and roll them back !

Our art teacher was framed by the police...

Our last math teacher was taken away...

Our music teacher never accepts notes from home...

Where do new teachers come from ?

They're produced on an assembly line !

Why did the teacher dress up like a cavewoman ?

To tell us about the after-school club !

Teacher - Is your father helping you with your homework ?

Pupil - No, sir, if anything he knows even less than I do !

Well, son, how did you find the mathematics exam ?

Unfortunately, it wasn't lost !

Teacher - Smith, give me a sentence with the word politics in it.

Smith - My pet parrot swallowed the alarm clock and now Polly ticks !

What's the best way to tell your teacher that you have forgotten to do your homework - again ?

From a great distance !

Teacher - If your father gave you 5 toys and your mother gave you 10 toys, what would you have ?

Pupil - Someone else's parents !

Why are fish smart ?

Because they travel in schools !

Teacher - Well, at least I know that no-one in the school tennis team will ever start smoking.

Principal - How do you work that out ?

Teacher - Because they always lose their matches !

Our School cook was arrested for cruelty - she was caught beating eggs, battering fish fingers, and whipping cream !

John - I bet our chemistry teacher could cure your insomnia...

John's Mother - Why, is he a doctor as well ?

John - No, but as soon as he starts to speak half the class fall asleep !

Teacher - Are you sending Gary to boarding school ?

Parent - Yes. His report says he is always bored !

★

Johnny -
Hey, Dad, I'll bet you can't write in the dark !

Dad -
Of course I can !

Johnny -
Good! I'll just turn out the light
and you can sign my school report !

Of course in my day we didn't have
computers to help us...

...we had to get our schoolwork
wrong all on our own !

I think Johnny will
make an excellent
astronaut in
later life...

Why do you think that ?

...because he's had
nothing but space
between his ears all the
years he's been at this
school !

Why are you taking Napoleon into your exams ?

It's a math exam, he's a ruler !

I would have done my homework, but...

I used up all the ink in my pen
drawing the curtains...

they didn't have any more copies of Romeo and
Juliet in the video library...

you said to hand it in tomorrow - and I will...

Which fruit do English teacher's
like best ?

The Grapes of Wrath !

Teacher -
Name a bird that wouldn't live in this
bird house.

Katy
- The Cuckoo.

Teacher -
That' right - how on earth did you
know that ?

Katy -
Everyone knows that
Cuckoos
live in clocks!

Did you hear about the
cross eyed teacher who
had to retire ?

He couldn't control
his pupils !

He must have been related to the
one-eyed teacher who
also had to retire...

...because he didn't
have enough pupils !

How many teachers does it take to
change a lightbulb ?

One if it's a free period, 17 if they're teaching !

Head -
I understand you're interested
in a career in languages ?

Pupil -
Yes, sir, my English teacher says
I speak perfect gobledygook!

What's the difference between a teacher and a
mouse ?

They're like chalk and cheese !

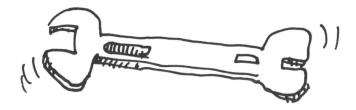

★
What part of the day does a robot teacher
look forward to ?

Assembly !

Why did you give an apple to our exchange werewolf teacher from Transylvania ?

Because I wanted to be creature's pet !

★

Our cookery teacher **grills** anyone who fails to hand in their homework...

Our gym teacher thinks we're all **good sports**...

Our music teacher makes a real **song and dance** when we're late for class...

★

Where do vampire teachers come from ?

Teacher Draining College !

★

Where do vampire teachers like to work ?

In the school necks door !

Teacher -
Have you been
stupid all your life ?

Pupil -
Not yet !

We have a new
Italian teacher -

I'll bet she pasta lot
of exams to get this
job !

What's the easiest way to get a day
off school ?

Wait until Saturday !

Teacher -
If you had 50 coins in each trouser
pocket, and 5 coins in each jacket pocket, what
would you have ?

Pupil -
Someone else's suit !

Pupil -
Do I need any qualifications to
work as a vet ?

Teacher -
No, you've had plenty of experience with
animals already - I've seen the rest of your
class !

Teacher -
The school cook has been caught wrapping
the eggs in blankets again!

Head -
What on earth was she doing that for ?

Teacher -
Because she wanted to serve coddled eggs !

I think you've been built upside down
Blenkinsop !
Why do you think that sir ?

Because your feet smell and your nose runs !

Teacher -
Why are you working out those multiplication problems on the floor ?

Pupil -
You told me not to use tables !

Teacher -
Why are you taking those running shoes into your exam ?

Pupil -
I'm hoping to jog my memory !

Teacher - How many letters in the alphabet ?

Pupil - 11 !

Teacher - How do you work that out ?

Pupil - t - h - e - a - l - p - h - a - b - e - t !

Head - Why do you want to take your science exam outside ?

Pupil - Because the truth is out there !

Teacher - Jenkins, what's the difference between a fairy tale and the excuses you give me for not doing your math homework ?

Jenkins - Don't know sir.

Teacher - A fairy tale is believable !

Why did the students eat their homework ?

Because the teacher said it was a piece of cake !

Here's your chemistry exam paper Blenkinsop - totally unhurt !

What do you mean totally unhurt ?

I mean there's not a mark on it !!

Why did the teacher have a pile of bricks on his head?

He wanted to build on his knowledge!

★

Why can you always believe what a teacher with a beard tells you?

They can't tell bare faced lies!

That new monster teacher is terrible – Jim was late yesterday and he bit his head off!

Did you hear about the cannibal teacher...

His pupils were all late, and now they're all ate!

I saw *my* history teacher in town last night...
...he was out on a date!
...his girlfriend is a history teacher as well...
...they go to a restaurant and talk about old times!

Knock,
Knock...

Knock, Knock...
Who's there ?
Giraffe...
Giraffe Who ?
Giraffe to sit in front of me
at this play ?

Knock, knock
Who's there ?
Amanda
Amanda who ?
Amanda last step - open the door !

Knock, knock
Who's there ?
Dell
Dell who ?
Dell never know I was here if you don't
tell them !

Knock, knock
Who's there ?
Toodle
Toodle who ?
Where are you going - I only just got here !

Knock, knock
Who's there ?
Paul
Paul who ?
Paul the door open and you'll see !

Knock Knock...
Who's there ?
Joanna...
Joanna who ?
Joanna stop asking stupid questions
and let me in !

Knock Knock...
Who's there ?
Ant...
Ant who ?
Ant I told you already ?

Knock Knock Knock...
Who's there ?
Moses...
Moses who ?
Moses if I knock 3 times you'll let me in !

Knock Knock...
Who's there ?
Tim...
Tim who ?
T-I-M-B-E-R !@*!!

Knock Knock...
Who's there ?
Kent...
Kent who ?
Kent you fix the doorbell ?

Knock Knock...
Who's there ?
Yul...
Yul who ?
Yul never know if you don't
open the door will you ? !

Knock Knock...
Who's there ?
Your arithmetic teacher...
hello...hello....Is anyone
there...?

Knock Knock...
Who's there ?
Isabel...
Isabel who ?
Isabel a legal requirement
on a bicycle ?

Knock Knock...
Who's there ?
Superman...
Superman who ?
You know I can't reveal my secret identity !

★

Knock Knock...
Who's there ?
Arfur...
Arfur who ?
Arfur got !

★

Knock Knock...
Who's there ?
CD...
CD who ?
CD guy on your front step ? That's me !

Knock Knock...
Who's there ?
Tish...
Tish who ?
Bless you !

Knock Knock...
Who's there ?
Hoo...
Who hoo ?
Are you an owl ?

Knock Knock...
Who's there ?
Snow...
Snow who ?
Snow use - I can't remember

Knock Knock...
Who's there?
Snow...
Snow who ?
Snow joke being out here
in the cold, let me in !

Knock Knock...
Who's there ?
Nona...
Nona who ?
Nona your business !

Knock Knock...
Who's there ?
Adolf...
Adolf who ?
Adolf ball hit me in de mouf !

Knock Knock...
Who's there ?
Alec...
Alec who ?
Alec to see you guess !

Knock Knock...
Who's there ?
Les...
Les who ?
Les cut the small talk - just open the door !

Knock Knock...
Who's there ?
Wendy...
Wendy who ?
Wendy red red robin goes bob bob
bobbin along...

Knock Knock...
Who's there ?
Guess...
Guess who ?
Wait, haven't we got this mixed up somehow ?

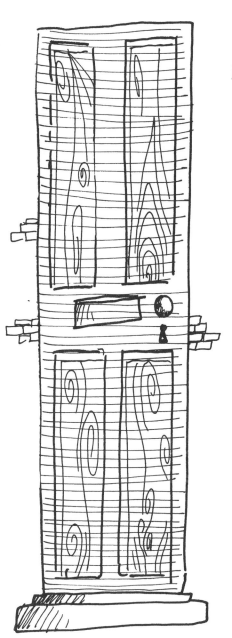

Knock Knock...
Who's there ?
Kungf...
Kungf who ?
No need to threaten
me !

Knock Knock...
Who's there ?
Marky...
Marky who ?
Markys stuck in the
keyhole,
can you open it
from your side ?

Knock Knock...
Who's there ?
Knock Knock...
Who's there ?
Knock Knock...
Just a minute I'll
open the door -
Yes, can I help you ?
I've called to
collect my new
hearing aid !

Knock Knock...
Who's there ?
Police...
Police who ?
Police let me in, I'm freezing out here !

Knock Knock...
Who's there ?
Pat...
Pat who ?
Actually it's Steve, I was just doing
an impersonation of Pat !

Knock Knock...
Who's there ?
Joe...
Joe who ?
Joe always have to
ask me that question ?

Knock Knock...
Who's there ?
The Cilla...
The Cilla who ?
The Cilla beggar who's
forgotten her key again !

Knock Knock...
Who's there ?
Geezer...
Geezer who ?
Geezer couple of minutes and
I'll pick this lock !

★

Knock, Knock...
Who's there ?
Carmen
Carmen who ?
Carmen to the front room and
look through the window !

★

Knock Knock...
Who's there ?
Jack...
Jack who ?
Jack my car up will you,
I want to fix the exhaust !

Knock Knock...
Who's there ?
L.E....
L.E. who ?
L.E. Funt !

Knock Knock...
Who's there ?
Kipper...
Kipper who ?
Kipper your hands off
my ice cream !

Knock Knock...
Who's there ?
Dinah...
Dinah who ?
Dinahsaur!

Knock Knock...
Who's there ?
Vlad...
Vlad who ?
Vlad a long time you take
to answer the door !

JINGLE
JINGLE

Knock Knock...
Who's there ?
Will...
Will who ?
Will you get these bells off my leg
- they're driving me crazy !

Knock Knock...
Who's there ?
Carl...
Carl who ?
Carl this a warm reception !?

Knock, Knock...
Who's there ?
Eddie
Eddie who ?
Eddie minute now I'm going to sneeze !

Knock Knock...
Who's there ?
Jess...
Jess who ?
Jess open the door will you !!

Knock, Knock...
Who's there ?
Iona
Iona who ?
Iona a house just like this one !

Knock Knock...
Who's there ?
Ivor...
Ivor who ?
Ivor good mind to leave if
you don't let me in !

Knock Knock...
Who's there ?
Apple...
Apple who ?
Apple the door
too hard and
hit myself in
the nose !

Knock Knock...
Who's there ?
Only Joe...
Only Joe who ?
Only Joking,
it's me really !

Knock, Knock...
Who's there ?
Fanny
Fanny who ?
Fanny how
you always
ask that
question ?!

Knock Knock...
Who's there ?
Cash...
Cash who ?
No thanks, I just had some peanuts !

Knock, Knock...
Who's there ?
Oscar
Oscar who ?
Oscar a silly question...

Knock Knock...
Who's there ?
Doris...
Doris who ?
Doris locked –
that's why I'm
knocking !

Knock Knock...
Who's there ?
Kurt...
Kurt who ?
Kurt out that last joke - it's terrible !

★

Knock Knock...
Who's there ?
Dennis...
Dennis who ?
Dennis *must* be
the right place - he
said *you'd*
ask that !

★

Knock Knock...
Who's there ?
Tinkerbell...
Tinkerbell who ?
Tinkerbell would save me having to
do all this knocking !

Knock Knock...
Who's there ?
Chester...
Chester who ?
Chester man delivering a parcel !

Knock Knock...
Who's there ?
A. Roland...
A. Roland who ?
A Roland butter
would be very nice -
do you have any !

Knock Knock...
Who's there ?
Ouvrez...
Ouvrez who ?
Ouvrez la porte, sil-te-plait !
(French pen-pal over for a visit)

Knock Knock...
Who's there ?
Gordon...
Gordon who ?
Gordon tired of standing
here I can tell you !

Knock Knock...
Who's there ?
Luke...
Luke who ?
Luke through the little
spyglass and you'll see !

Knock Knock...
Who's there ?
June...
June who ?
June know how long I've
been waiting out here ?!

Knock Knock...
Who's there ?
Creatures from another dimension...
Creatures from another dimension who ?
Creatures from another dimension who are
getting tired of waiting to be let in, earthling !

Knock Knock...
Who's there ?
Witch Doctor...
Witch Doctor who ?
The one in the floppy
hat and long scarf !

Knock Knock...
Who's there ?
Ooh Ooh Ooh...
Ooh Ooh Ooh who ?
Stop playing at fire engines and let me in !

Knock Knock...
Who's there ?
Len...
Len who ?
Len me a key and I
won't have to knock
any more !

Animal Antics...

Looks like Reindeer !

What do you call a goat who robs banks ?

Billy the Kid !

If cows get milked - what do goats get ?

Butted !

*If a house mouse sleeps in a house
and a field mouse sleeps in a field
do dormice sleep in dorms ?*

Where do deer go when they want something to read ?

Buck Shops !

Rabbit - How do I know this TV will work when I get it home ?

Shopkeeper -It comes with a full Warrenty !

Why do elephants
paint their toenails
red ?

So they can hide in
Cherry trees !

Hickory Dickory Dock,
The horse ran up the clock.

Anybody need any firewood ?

Why is the sky so high ?

So birds don't bump their heads !

What's the difference between a flea and
a wolf ?

One prowls on the hairy and the other howls
on the prairie !

When Mary had a little lamb
The doctor was surprised
But when Old Macdonald had a farm
He couldn't believe his eyes !

What do you give an elephant that's feeling sick ?

Plenty of room !

What do you get if you
cross a cow with a camel ?

A lumpy custard pie !

How do you stop rabbits digging up your garden ?

Easy - take their tools away !

What was the title of the Shakespeare play about pigs ?

Hamlet !

We call our dog Locksmith because every now and again he makes a bolt for the door !

Why are you taking that snake into the mathematics exam ?

It's an adder !

How many elephants can you get into a car ?

Four. 2 in the front seats and 2 in the back seats !

How many hippos can you get into a car ?

Four ?

Don't be silly ! There are 4 elephants in it already !

Amateur Lion Taming

by

Claude Bottom

What do you call an elephant in a telephone booth ?

Whatever you like - it will be stuck so it can't chase you !

What goes 'Mark, Mark...'

A dog with a swollen lip !

What are baby crabs called ?

Nippers !

Waiter - Bring me a crocodile sandwich....
....and make it snappy !

Did you hear about the Shetland Pony who was asked to leave the animal choir ?

She was always a little horse !

Police are looking for a criminal octopus...

He is well armed and dangerous !

What lies at the bottom of the sea
and shivers ?

A nervous wreck !

What's the fastest fish in the lake ?

A motor Pike !

HUMAN BEANS IN TOMATO SAUCE

What does your cat
eat for breakfast ?

**Mine eats Mice
Crispies !**

Did you know that
alligators eat beans
for lunch ?

**Human Beans of
course !**

Noah's Ark was able to find its way about at night because it had been fitted with floodlights !

Why do bees hum ?

Because they have forgotten the words !

Where do you take an injured bee ?

To the waspital !

...just as you would take an injured pony to the horsepital !

★

Why do station porters like elephants ?

Because they always carry their own trunks !

What has 10 legs, 3 heads, but only 2 arms ?

A man and a dog sitting on a zebra !

What is large and zooms through the jungle at tremendous speeds ?

An elephant on a motor bike !

Why should you never play cards for money in the jungle ?

Because there are too many Cheetahs about !

What vegetable do you get if you cross a sheepdog with a bunch of daffodils ?

A collie - flower !

Why is the sky blue ?

So birds know they're not flying upside down !

Why do elephants paint the soles of
their feet yellow ?

So they can hide upside down in custard !

Hickory Dickory Dock,
Three mice ran up the clock.

The clock struck one...
...the other two got out of the
way just in time !

What did the dog say when it sat on some
sandpaper ?

Ruff !

What is the correct name for a water otter ?

A kettle !

What did the Pink Panther say when he stood on an ant ?

Dead ant, dead ant, dead ant dead ant dead ant...

Mary had a little lamb
she also had a horse
for the horse
she made a saddle
for the lamb
she made mint sauce !

BURP...

Why do elephants have trunks ?

Because they'd look funny with a suitcase !

When is it bad luck to have a
black cat cross your path ?

When you are a mouse !

What is the difference between an apple and
an elephant ?

Apples are green !

★

What's the best way to catch a mouse ?

Get someone to throw one at you !

How many elephants does it take to change a lightbulb?

Four! One to hold the bulb and three to turn the stepladder!

What lives on a ship and says 'croak, croak!' when it's foggy?

A Froghorn!

What do you call a delinquent octopus?

A crazy, mixed -up squid!

What went wrong with the mouse's comedy routine?

The audience thought it was too cheesy!

Is it true that you can speak in cat language?

Me - How?

Did you hear about the 4 elephants who bought a new car so they could play the game they like best... ?

...squash !

Did you hear about the boy whose kite wouldn't work ?

He'd made it out of flypaper !

What is the most cowardly farmyard creature ?

The Chicken !

★

What do you call two pigs that live together ?

Pen pals !

Why did the porcupine cross the road ?

He was searching for the point in life !

What is the highest form
of animal life ?

A giraffe !

What do you do if
an elephant sits in front
of you at the play ?

Miss the play !

What do you call a horse that sunbathes
behind a venetian blind ?

A zebra !

What do you call a nervous insect ?

A jitterbug !

Why couldn't the butterfly get into
the dance ?

Because it was a moth ball !

What do you get if you cross a giraffe and a dog ?

An animal that chases low flying
planes instead of cars !

What is the difference
between a skunk
and a squirrel ?

Skunks don't know how to
operate a deodorant spray !

What do you call a vicious animal that
devours your relatives ?

An anteater !

Your dog must be really intelligent
if he can play scrabble!

Nah! He never wins !

What animal do you
eat for dessert ?

Moose !

Why did the duck cross the
highway at rush hour ?

I don't know, it must have
been quackers !

What is the most
valuable fish ?

The goldfish !

What does an elephant say when answering
the phone ?

I'm all ears !

What weighs a lot and wears flowers in its hair ?

A Hippy - potamous !

Where do animals go when they get some free time ?

They fly jumbo jets to Moo York !

What is green and very dangerous ?

A 12 bore cucumber !

What did the chicken say when the farmer grabbed it by the tail feathers ?

Oh, No! This is the end of me !!

What is a kangaroo's best-loved cowboy hero ?

Hopalong Cassidy !

What playground game do kangaroos prefer ?

Hopscotch !

Monster Madness...

Eat your vegetables, they'll help
your complexion.

But I don't want green cheeks !

What do vampires buy every week ?

The Clottery Tickets !

What should you take if a monster
invites you for dinner ?

Someone who can't run as fast as you !

Why do vampires have to
write so many letters ?

They have to reply to their
fang mail !

What sort of monster cooks you a tasty
breakfast each morning ?

A mummy !

Why are ghosts so bad at telling lies ?

Because you can always see through them !

The Haunted House

by

Hugo First

Mummy, what is a vampire ?

Be quiet dear and drink your blood before it clots !

What do you call a
tall, evil, green,
hairy monster ?

Whatever he tells you to !

Which handicraft do monsters love ?

Tie and Die !

Which game do monsters love best ?

Hide and Shriek !

Did you see that wolf ?

Where ?

No, it was just an ordinary one !

What did the monster's parents say when he agreed to wash the dishes ?

That's the spirit !

It's no good locking your door - monsters can always get in !

They have a set of skeleton keys !

Doctor, said the cannibal, I have this terrible stomach ache !

You must have eaten someone who disagreed with you !

A vampire's coffin fell off the back of a truck and started rolling down a steep hill. The vampire knew exactly what to do. He went into a local drugstore and asked if they had any sore throat sweets to stop his coffin !

Where do vampires keep their savings ?

In a blood bank !

Did you hear about the baby monster who had hundreds of little holes all over his face ?

He was learning to eat with a fork !

Why do vampires take their football so seriously ?

Because there is always so much at stake !

Where do ghosts learn to frighten people ?

At swooniversity !

What do ghosts write their letters on?

Type - frighters !

How do mummies keep a secret ?

They keep it under wraps !

What do you call a monster who never blows his nose ?

The bogeyman !

Why do skeletons rub themselves all over with towels when they've been swimming ?

To get bone dry !

Which fast food do sea monsters love ?

Fish and ships

What do you call a nervous witch ?

A twitch !

Menu

Sean cocktail

or

Dawn on the cob

followed by

I scream !
(and so would you if you had been there !)

What's the difference between a monster after
a meal and some scrambled eggs ?

One is full of yolks, the other full of folks !

What sort of horses do monsters ride?

Night mares !

When a monster's hungry and needs to be fed,
it's no good hiding under the bed !
He'll roll you in the mattress,
till you're buried like a mole,
then chomp you down in two big bites,
like a giant jelly roll !

Why was the monster's head sticky ?

Because he styled his hair with a honey comb !

What did the monster say when it saw someone
going past on a mountain bike ?

Ah ! Meals on wheels !

What soup did the vampire choose at
the restaurant ?

Scream of mushroom !

Monster - Waiter, this is ordinary spaghetti
- I ordered worms !

Waiter - Ah, I wondered why the man on the
table next to you was turning green
and groaning !

Sally - What is the difference between a
monster and a piece of toast ?

Jim - I don't know.

Sally - Have you ever tried dunking a
monster in a hot drink ?

Why did the monster have twins in his lunchbox ?

In case he wanted seconds !

I'd tell you the story of the vampire's broken tooth...

...but there's no point !

Why aren't robots afraid of monsters ?

Because they have nerves of steel !

Did you hear about the witch who was caught speeding on her broomstick ?

She had a brush with the law !

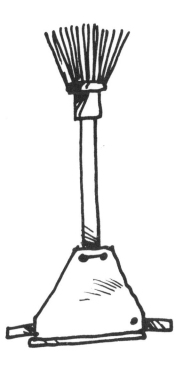

What shape does a monster love to draw ?

A vicious circle !

What do you think when
you see a monster ?

'I hope he hasn't
seen me !'

Where do monsters send
their dirty washing ?

The dry screamers !
and they send it in a hauntry basket !

★

How do skeletons
know when the
weather is going
to change ?

They can feel it in
their bones !

What do monsters read in the newspaper
every morning ?

Their horror - scope !

What do you call a monster
with a wooden leg ?

Long John Slither !

What did the *mummy
monster* say to her child
at the dining table ?

**Don't spook with your
mouth full !**

What do baby monsters sometimes
suffer from ?

Chicken spooks !

Why did the monster buy a guillotine ?

Because he wanted to get ahead in life !

Why do vampire families never fight ?

Because they can't stand bad blood !

Where do ghosts read the news ?

In a whhhooooosspaper !

What do ghosts leave their children when they die ?

All their unwordly goods !

What sort of music do mummies like best ?

Wrap music !

What do you call a vampire who spends all his time drinking beer ?

Count Drunkula !

Why do skeletons not trust archaeologists ?

Because they indulge in skullduggery !

Which toy do sea monsters love ?

A sea-saw !

Gnomes have dreadful table manners...

...they are always Goblin their food !

Why are monsters so horrible ?

It's in the blood !

*A werewolf can't die
a vampire can fly
a monster can bite off your head.
It's no wonder I'm scared'
for the noise I just heard...*

means they're all hiding under my bed !

Which people in ancient Rome did monsters
love best ?

Glad He Ate Us !

What is the best way to let a vampire know
he's not welcome at your party ?

Offer him a garlic sausage sandwich in a hot
cross bun, and tell him there is stake to follow !

What was the ghost put in jail for ?

Driving without due scare and attention !

What sort of pets do monsters keep ?

Ghould - fish !

What do monsters make
with cars ?

Traffic jam !

What songs do they
play at ghostly
discos ?

Haunting melodies !

What games do bats like to play on Halloween ?

Anything with a ball !

Why was the vampire asked to leave the
orchestra ?

His bite was even worse than his Bach !

Sally - Did you make a sandwich with half a monster in it?

Jim - certainly not!

Sally - Oh! Then you must have eaten half already!

★

How can you help a starving monster?

Give him a hand!

★

How does a werewolf sign his letters?

Best vicious!

★

Why do monsters let out a blood curdling scream?

Because otherwise it would be too runny to spread on their sandwiches!

What do monsters take
to a house warming party ?

Matches !

What game do
ghostly mice play at
parties ?

Hide and Squeak !

What magazine do houseproud
monsters read ?

Ghouled Housekeeping !

Why does Cinderella play football so badly ?

**Well, so would you if you had
a pumpkin for a coach !**

A goblin lost his left arm in an accident.

I hear he's all right now !

Fishy Foolishness...

Which fish runs the undersea mafia?

The Codfather!

Why are Herrings such healthy fish ?

**Because you never see them ill,
only cured !**

What sort of fish go to heaven when they die ?

Angel fish !

*Roses are red,
violets are blue,
you look like a
trout,and you
smell like one
too !*

*If you use a skunk to catch fish you always
catch them hook, line and stinker !*

★

Which food can you buy at the stand next
to the power station ?

Nuclear fission chips !

Which sea creatures do you need for
a game of fish ?

Prawns !

★

Where do dolphins learn ?

In Schools, of course !

★

Where do baby fish go ?

To Plaice-school !

★

What would you order at the
pirate restaurant ?

Pizzas of eight !

Why do fish dream of mountain climbing?

They'd love to scale the heights!

Why was the jellyfish trembling so much?

He had no backbone!

Why don't fish like basketball?

They're afraid of the net!

★

Knock, knock...
Who's there?
Plaice...
Plaice who?
Plaice let me in,
I'm wet through!

Why was the beach wet ?

Because the sea weed !

Why are some
shellfish always bad
tempered ?

They can't help it -
they were born
crabby !

Where do fish like going every summer ?

Finland !

How do fish know exactly
what everything weighs ?

They always have a set
of scales on them !

What do sharks eat at parties ?

Fish-cakes
Jelly-fish
and
Sandwiches

Where do whales get
weighed ?

At a whale - weigh
station !

What do fish drink ?

Water of course, they can't use bottle openers
!

★

What do fish use
to stop getting
sunburned ?

Sun tan ocean !

Which fish do pirates
wear on their belts ?

Swordfish !

Who are the worst
criminals in the lake ?

River bank robbers !

Which jewels do lady
fish wear ?

Eel-rings !

Which is the strongest
sea creature ?

The muscle !

Who does all the woodwork in the sea ?

Plankton !

How do fish pass the long winter evenings ?

They tell each other tails !

What did the sea say to the beach ?

It didn't say anything - it waved !

Where do fish keep their savings ?

In the river bank !

What do you call a whale in the
Sahara desert ?

Lost !

Why did the fisherman's wife take her son to
the doctor's ?

Because he had a bad haddock !

Where would you find a pilot whale ?

On board a flying fish !

★

Two men were walking along in the desert. One said to the other "This is a lovely sandy beach." The other replied "Yes, but the tide is a heck of a long way out !"

What do fish do for adventure ?

They scale mountains !

How do vampire fish communicate ?

With wails !

Roses are red,
violets are pink,
there's an octopus in
the bathtub,
so I'll get washed in
the sink !

Why do you suck your maggots before putting
them on the hook ?

So I can wait for the fish with baited breath !

What sort of fish never have any money ?

Poor - poises !

What do you give a deaf fish ?

A herring aid !

What do fish do when the TV breaks down ?

Send for the electric eel !

Which fish are best for freezing ?

Skates !

What's the mushy stuff between a shark's teeth ?

Slow swimmers !

★

What sort of music do dolphins prefer ?

Sole music !

What do sharks
call people
who fall off
speedboats ?

Fast food !

Why don't sharks eat people in submarines ?

They don't like canned food !

Why are the people at the
fish counter so unpleasant ?

Because their job makes
them sell fish !

What is the best way to
get a message to a fish ?

Drop it a line !

What fish can perform
operations ?

A sturgeon !

Who was the most notorious cowboy fish ?

Billy the Squid !

Why was the kipper sent
to jail ?

Because he was gill - ty !

What do you get if you cross a herd of
elephants with a school of fish ?

Swimming trunks !

What do you give to a deaf sea nymph ?

A Mermaid !

What sort of
fish like to work
fingers to
the bone ?

Piranha Fish !

Where do fish sleep ?

On a sea bed !

What sort of trout can you see after a
thunderstorm ?

A Rainbow !

What did the Inuit sing at suppertime ?

" Whale Meat Again..."

What did the mother whale say to the
cry-baby whale ?

Stop blubbering !

What game do
young fish play at
parties ?

Sardines !

Batty Brain Teasers...

Why did the man order alphabet soup ?

He wanted to eat his words !

What were the gangster's last words ?

"Who put the violin in my violin case ?"

What is the name of the detective who solves all his crimes by pure accident ?

Sheer - Luck Holmes !

What is the one thing you can catch with your hands tied ?

A cold !

Who invented the steam engine ?

No he didn't, it was Watt !

Why are dentists so miserable ?

Because they are always looking down in the mouth !

Why are men with beards more honest ?

Because they can't tell bare-faced lies !

What do you get if you drop a
piano down a coal mine ?

A flat minor !

What's the best thing to put into a pie ?

Your knife and fork !

Which is the strongest thing in the garden ?

The muscle sprout !

And which is the weakest ?

The weeds !

What do you get if you cross a toy bear
with a pig ?

A teddy boar !

Waiter, there's a fly in my soup !

**Don't worry, I'll give you a reduction for the
soup he eats!**

Why do elephants wear green jackets ?

**So they can walk across a pool table without
being seen !**

Where would you find a floppy trumpet ?

In a rubber band !

Where does tea come from ?

In between the letters S and U !

What starts at the bottom and goes all the way down to the floor ?

Your leg !

Who invented fire ?

Some bright spark !

How do you start a teddy bear race ?

Ready, Teddy, Go !

What did the baby chick say when she saw a bottle of champagne ?

Shell we have a drink ?

What gets bigger the more you take out of it ?

A hole !

How do you make a Swiss roll ?

Push him down an alp !

Little dog,
crossing street,
motor car,
sausage meat !

What sort of music was invented by cave men ?

Rock music !

What happened to the man who stole
a truck load of prunes ?

He was on the run for months !

Waiter, there's a fly in my soup !

**Thank you for telling me, sir,
I'd forgotten to charge you for it !**

How do you get rid of a boomerang ?

Throw it down a one-way street !

What's black and white and red all over ?

A newspaper !

How does the snow queen travel about ?

By icicle !

How do you get down from a giraffe ?

You don't get down from a giraffe - you get down from a duck !

What goes zzub, zzub ?

A bee flying the wrong way !

Why do cows moo ?

Because their horns don't work !

What sport does Dracula love watching on TV ?

Bat-minton !

How do you make a
Venetian blind ?

Poke him in the eyes !

What kind of nuts get
launched into outer space ?

Astronuts !

What sort of music do
miners like to listen to ?

Rock and coal !

Mary had a little lamb,
it's fleece was black as soot,
and everywhere that Mary went,
its sooty foot it put !

What do they call the back entrance to a cafeteria ?

The bacteria !

Where do Inuits train their dogs ?

The mushroom !

Why did Tarzan jump onto the vine ?

He wanted to get into the swing of things !

Why did the doll blush ?

Because she saw the teddy bare !

How do you know when it's been raining cats and dogs ?

There are lots of little poodles on the pavement !

What do you call a cat with 8 legs ?

An octopus !

What do Inuits eat for breakfast ?

Ice Crispies !

Where would you find a dog with 4 broken legs ?

Wherever you left it !

Why do potatoes always know what you've done ?

Because they have eyes !

What's the difference between a butcher and a night watchman ?

One weighs a steak, the other stays awake !

★

Have you ever seen a Duchess ?

Yes, it's just like an English "s" !

★

How many days of the week begin with T ?

All except Sunday, when I have coffee !

★

Where does Dracula go when he visits New York ?

The Vampire State Building !

In which battle was Alexander the Great killed?

His last one !

Why did the elephant refuse to play cards
with his two friends ?

**Because one of them was lion and
the other was a cheetah !**

Where did Noah keep all

the elderly bees ?

In his Ark-hives !

Why did the orchestra have such bad manners ?

**They didn't know how to conduct
themselves !**

What goes up a drainpipe but can't come down
a drainpipe ?

An umbrella !

Good morning Mr
Butcher, do you have a
sheep's head?

No - it's just the way
part my hair!

I

★

Caveman chasing dinosaurs
wants to make a bronto burger
hungry T Rex joins in too...
...hope he enjoyed his human stew!

★

What do you call someone who is always
working overtime?

A clock mender!

★

Good morning sir,
can I interest you
in a pocket calculator?

No, thanks, I
already know how
many pockets
I've got!

When do 2 and 2 make more than 4 ?

When they make 22 !

Why do mother kangaroos
hate rainy days ?

**Because the children have to play
indoors when it rains !**

How can you sleep like a log ?

Put your bed in the fireplace !

What can you catch and hold but never
touch ?

Your breath !

What is yellow and costs millions ?

**A banana - I lied about it
costing millions !**

Why do vampires use more toothpaste than ordinary people ?

They have bat breath !

What happens when a frog breaks down ?

He gets toad away !

What is green and goes round and round ?

An alien in a washing machine !

Where was the American declaration of Independence signed ?

At the bottom !

PLEASE SIGN HERE ...

Why do bees buzz ?

Because they don't know how to whistle !

Why did the stupid
robber carry
two bricks ?

Because the bank
windows were
double glazed !

My friend is so thin that when
we go to the park
the ducks throw bread at him !

Why did the jogger need
so many hankies ?

Because his nose was
always running !

What animal uses a nutcracker ?

A squirrel with no teeth !

Why was the soccer
field soggy ?

Because the
players were
always dribbling !

What do you give to
injured fruit ?

Lemonade !

What do gardeners eat for breakfast ?

Shredded weed !

What do cats eat for breakfast ?

Shredded tweet !

Why did the man jump up and down
after taking his medicine ?

Because he forgot to shake the bottle
before he took it !

Medical Mayhem...

Doctor, doctor, I think I'm invisible !

Who said that ?

Doctor, doctor, I think I'm a pair of curtains !

Pull yourself together !

Doctor, doctor, my wife thinks she's
a motorbike !

Give her two of these pills and she'll be cured !

But how will I get home then ?

Doctor, doctor, I'm shrinking !

Well, you'll just have to be a little patient !

Doctor, doctor, my wife thinks she's a chicken !

Do you want me to cure her ?

No, I just wondered if you had any good egg recipes !

Doctor, doctor, everyone keeps ignoring me !

Next patient please !

Doctor, doctor, I think I'm a playing card !

You'll just have to deal with it yourself !

Doctor, doctor, I think I'm a mousetrap !

Snap out of it !

Doctor, doctor, all my friends think I'm a liar !

I find that hard to believe !

Doctor, doctor, I keep thinking that my parents are goats !

When did you start to have these thoughts ?

When I was a kid !

I SENT HIM HOME TO FETCH HIS NANNY!

Doctor, doctor, I think I'm becoming invisible !

I'm sorry, I can't see you now !

Doctor, doctor, I can't seem to get to sleep at night !

Sleep on the windowsill, you'll soon drop off !

Doctor, doctor, I have a lot of wind, can you give me anything for it?

Certainly, here's a kite!

Doctor, doctor, my hair is falling out, have you anything to keep it in?

Try this paper bag!

Doctor, doctor, you know those pills you gave me for a headache - well they worked. Now can you give me something to take the headache away!

Doctor, doctor, I think I'm a mosquito!

Go away, sucker!

Doctor, doctor, I'm boiling up !

Just simmer down !

Nurse, nurse, I need to see a doctor !

Which doctor?

No, just an ordinary one !

HE'S PAYING!

Doctor, doctor, I think I have a split personality !

In that case I will have to charge you double !

Doctor, doctor, I'm a little hoarse !

I'll be with you in a minute - just take your saddle off and relax !

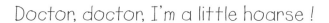

Doctor, doctor, I swallowed
a spoon !

**Just sit there quietly
and don't stir !**

Doctor, doctor, I've lost
my memory !

*That's terrible. When did
you first notice ?*

When did I notice what ?

Doctor, doctor, I think I'm a dog !

*Well, fetch this stick then roll over
and let me tickle your tummy !*

Will that cure me ?

**No, but I was never allowed to
have a pet as a child !**

Doctor, doctor, I think I have a split personality !

I'm sorry, one of you will have to wait outside !

Doctor, doctor, my wife wants to know if you can stop me being so argumentative ?

I'm sorry Mr. Brown, there's nothing I can do !

Yes there is !

I'm not feeling myself today, so can you ask the doctor to call round and see Mr. Smith instead !

Doctor, doctor, I keep thinking that I have been here before !

Oh. It's you again !

Doctor, doctor, can you help me to stop smoking ?

Well, you could try not setting fire to your clothes !

Doctor, doctor, can you give me a sick note
to get a week off school ?

You look perfectly healthy to me !

Yes, but I'm sick of going to school !

Doctor, doctor, I've just swallowed a tin of
gloss paint !

**Yes, my receptionist said you'd taken a
shine to her !**

Doctor, doctor my wife just buried
my radio in the garden !

Why did she do that ?

The batteries were dead !

Doctor, doctor, I've got
athlete's
foot in my head !

What makes you think that ?

Because my nose keeps running !

Doctor, doctor, there's a man at the surgery door with a wooden leg !

Tell him to hop it !

Doctor, doctor, the doctor says these pills you prescribed me are for cows !

Well, you said you wanted to be as strong as an ox !

Doctor, doctor, I keep seeing numbers in front of my eyes all the time !

Take two of these pills every night !

Will I ever be cured ?

I wouldn't count on it !

Doctor, doctor, I keep seeing spots
in front of my eyes !

Have you seen an optician !

No, just the spots !

Doctor, doctor, people are saying that you're
a vampire !

Nonsense ! Necks please !

Doctor, doctor, I keep stealing things from
electrical shops !

**Take these pills twice a day, and if they don't
work bring me a CD player next time you come !**

Doctor, doctor, wherever I
go I hear this ringing
in my ears !

**I'm not surprised, you
always wear
bell bottoms !**

Doctor, doctor, I'm worried that I'm a burglar !

Well, have you taken anything for it ?

Doctor, doctor, why are you
so short tempered ?

I don't have enough patients !

Doctor, doctor, three beer kegs have
just fallen on me ?

Don't worry, it was light ale !

Doctor, doctor, I think I'm turning
into a mummy !

Hmmm, better keep well wrapped up !

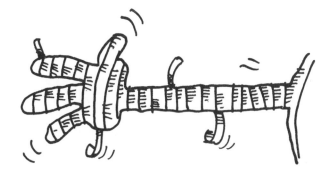

Doctor, doctor, I think I need some antibiotics !

Why, are you feeling ill ?

No, but my auntie feels terrible !

★

Doctor, doctor, I think I've caught a computer virus !

I've warned you before about eating chips !

★

Doctor, doctor... I've not stopped laughing since my operation !

Well, I told you the surgeon would have you in stitches !

★

Doctor, doctor... Did you hear about the appendix who went out and bought a new suit – because he heard that the doctor was going to take him out !

Doctor, doctor, I have
these little flowers
growing out of my feet !

It's all right, they're
just corn flowers !

Doctor, doctor, how can I stop my
nose running ?

Stick your foot out and trip it up !

Ah, Mr. Smith, did you drink your medicine after
your bath like I asked you to ?

No doctor, after I had drunk the bath I had no
room for the medicine !

Doctor, doctor...
You don't really think I'm turning into a
grandfather clock do you ?

No, I was just winding you up !

★

Nurse, nurse, will the doctor be around soon?

No, he'll be tall and slim as usual!

Doctor, doctor, after the operation will I be able to play the piano?

Of course Mr. Blenkinsop!

That's brilliant - because I can't now!

Doctor, doctor, I'm suffering from terrible insomnia!

Oh! I'm sure all you need is a good night's sleep!

Doctor, doctor, I only have one tooth, what should I do?

You'll just have to grin and bare it!

Doctor, doctor, my husband keeps dressing
up like a French soldier !

Another case of Legionnaires disease !

Doctor, doctor, I need you to recommend
a good plastic surgeon !

Why, what do you need done ?

**Well, I put the TV too close to the fire
and it's melted !**

Doctor, doctor, I've started having dizzy spells !

When do they start ?

Whenever I step off the merry-go-round !

Doctor, doctor...
I have a fish hook stuck
in the side of
my mouth !

**I thought you were
waiting to see me
with baited breath !**

Doctor, doctor, can you help
me to lose weight ?

**Well, you could lose half your weight
straight away !**

How on earth do I do that ?

Put down those shopping bags !

Doctor, doctor, I've just swallowed some coins ?

Why on earth did you do that !

**I was feeling ill, and I thought the change
would do me good !**

Doctor, doctor, what
is good for a
headache ?

**Banging your
head against
a wall works
every time !**

Doctor, doctor, I've just been bitten by a snake - do you think there is any chance of an infection ?

I wouldn't have thought so, snakes are pretty resilient creatures !

Doctor, doctor, my snoring is driving the folks next door crazy !

Well, maybe you should sleep in your own home from now on !

Doctor, doctor, my pig has pimples, what should I give him ?

Try this oinkment !

Doctor, doctor... I swallowed a bone !

Are you choking ?

No, I really did !

Crazy Crosses...

What do you get if you cross your dad's sister with an Inuit ?

Auntie freeze !

What do you get if you cross a kangaroo with a snowman?

A ski jumper !

★

What do you get if you cross a cow with a trampoline ?

A milkshake !

★

What do you get if you cross a road without looking ?

Knocked down, stupid !

★

What do you get if you cross a frog with a rabbit ?

A bunny ribbit !

★

What do you get if you cross a cat with a parrot ?

A carrot !

What do you get if you cross a film director
and a horse drawn vehicle ?

Orson Kart !

★

What do you get
if you cross
a bear with a
cow pat ?

Winnie the Pooh !

★

What do you get if you cross a chicken with a
skunk ?

A fowl smell !

★

What do you get if you cross a fly with a
detective ?

A police insector !

★

What do you get if you cross a cow with a
thief ?

A beef burglar !

What do you get if you cross a pig with an ambulance ?

A Hambulance !

What do you get if you cross
a window cleaner with a giraffe ?

A window cleaner who doesn't
need any ladders !

What do you
get if you
cross a pig
with Dracula ?

A Hampire !

What do you get if you cross a chicken
with someone who tells jokes ?

A comedihen !

What do you get if you cross a lizard with a baby ?

A creepy crawler !

What do you get if you cross a bucket of coal with a spacecraft ?

Rocket fuel !

What do you get if you cross hockey equipment with hiking gear ?

A pucksack !

What do you get if you cross a pig with a mathematical quantity ?

A pork pi !

What do you get if you cross a goldfish
bowl with a TV ?

Tele-fish-ion !

What do you get if you cross an explorer with
a cat ?

Christopher Col**umpuss** !

What do you get if
you cross a cowboy
with
a dinosaur ?

Tyrannosaurus Tex !

What do you get if you cross a dessert
with an ape ?

Lemon meringue-utan pie !

What do you get if you cross the mafia
and a box of teaspoons ?

A gangstir !

What do you get if you cross a river with a broken bridge ?

Very, very wet !

What do you get if you cross a tree with a fruit ?

A Pineapple !

What do you get if you cross a mathematics teacher with anything ?

A mathematics teacher !

Now...

TURN TO PAGE 46 OF YOUR HARD MATHS BOOK !

What do you get if you cross a pony with a TV detective ?

Inspector Horse !

What do you get if you cross a famous detective and a lot of good fortune ?

Sheer luck Holmes !

What do you get if you cross a grizzly bear
with a harp ?

A bare-faced lyre !

What do you get if you cross a mouse
and an elephant ?

An animal that's scared to look in the mirror !

What do you
get if you
cross a dog
with someone
worried about
something ?

Nervous Rex !

What do you get if you cross a duck and
a TV show ?

A Duckumentary !

What do you get if you cross an elephant with a large bottle of champagne ?

Drunk and disorderly !

What do you get if you cross a pig with a centipede ?

Bacon and legs !

What do you get if you cross kitchen equipment with a vampire ?

Count spatula !

What do you get if you cross a poodle with a hen ?

Pooched eggs !

What do you get if you cross an octopus and a hen ?

Enough drumsticks for everyone !

★

What do you get if you cross a crocodile and a lion ?

I don't know, but I hope it doesn't move in next door !

★

What do you get if you cross a box of hankies with a cold ?

A - A - A -tishoo

★

What game do you get if you cross frogs' legs and bagpipes ?

Hop scotch !

What do you get if you cross a scary
story and a dog ?

Someone who is terrier - fied !

What do you get if you cross a bee with a bell ?

A hum dinger !

What do you get if you cross a Star Wars
robot with a sheep ?

R 2 D ewe !

★

What do you get
if you cross a
great invention
with some herbs ?

**A thyme
machine !**

What do you get if you cross a window
with a guillotine ?

A pane in the neck !

What do you get if you cross a carrier
pigeon and a wodpecker ?

**A bird that knocks before delivering the
message !**

What do you get if you cross a sore throat
and some Christmas decorations ?

Tinselitis !

What do you get if you cross a mouse
with a can opener ?

**Something that can get the cheese from the
refrigerator without even opening the door !**

What do you get if you cross a wizard
and an hot-air balloon ?

A flying sorcerer !

What do you get if you cross a sheep with a
discount store ?

Lots of baaaaagains !

What do you get if you cross a James Bond
movie and a soccer player ?

Goal - finger !

What do you get if you
cross a ghost
and an optician ?

Spook - tacles !

What do you get if you
cross a giant
monopoly set with a
safari guide ?

A big game hunter !

What do you get if
you cross a man
inside your TV set and
someone very brainy ?

In - tele - gent !

What do you get
when teenage aliens
have a party ?

A space racket !

★

What do you get if
you cross a piece
of luggage and some
stolen goods ?

A case of robbery !

★

What do you get if you cross a hammock
and a dog ?

A rocker spaniel !

★

What do you get if
you draw dots
and dashes on
your hanky ?

A code in the
nose !

What do you get if you cross a hive of bees
with a knitting pattern for mittens ?

Nice and swarm !

What do you get if you cross a dog
with a tree ?

Something with a completely silent bark !

What do you get if you cross a French and a
German fortune telling device ?

A oui - ja board !

What do you get if you cross a parrot with
a shark ?

An animal that talks your head off !

What do you get if you cross a
computer with a beefburger ?

A Big Mac !

What do you get if you cross a coat and
a fire ?

A blazer !

What do you get if you cross a waiter
and a slippery floor ?

Flying saucers !

What do get when you cross an angry young
man and someone who can't decide which of
his 20 shoes to wear ?

a ten pair tantrum !

What do you get if
you cross a cow and a
moped ?

A mooter scooter !

What do you get if you cross
a painting and a rodent ?

A mouse - terpiece !

What do you get if you cross the African
jungle with a map of Toronto ?

Completely lost !

What do you get
if you cross a
portable stereo
and a pig ?

An MPig3 player !

What do you get if you
cross two vampire
natives ?

Blood brothers !

Leisure Laughs...

Our teacher is going
to the Bahamas this Summer !

Jamaica ?

No, she wanted to go !

When we went on a trip last year - the plane was so old...

...it had solid tires !

...the 2 previous owners were the Wright Brothers !

...one of the seats said "Reserved for Julius Caesar" !

...the co-pilot had to keep running to the tail to rewind the motor !

...the seats were covered in dinosaur hide !

...the pilot was taught to fly by Baron Von Richtofen !

Who always gets the sack on his first day at work ?

Santa Claus !

Dear Santa...

If I'm good
it's understood
that you'll bring me
a new CD.

If I'm kind
I know I'll find
a guitar to play
on Christmas Day.

So from now on,
You're going to find,
that I'll be helpful,
good and kind,
and I intend to stay
that way !
At least, that is, till the
very next day !

Passenger- I'm nervous, I've never
flown before ?

Hostess- Oh, don't you start, I've got enough
trouble with the pilot !

171

What do you call two girls with Christmas decorations on their heads ?

Holly and Ivy !

Where do snowmen go to dance ?

Snowballs !

What do you call someone who casts spells at the seaside ?

A Sandwitch !

Two elephants wanted to go swimming at the pool but they couldn't - they only had one pair of trunks between them !

★

What do you call a man with a hoe and a spade on his head ?

Doug !

How did you find your steak sir?

Easy, I just moved these two fries and there it was!

Waiter ! This egg is bad !

That's not my fault. I only laid the table !

How does a vampire cross the sea ?

In a blood vessel !

★

How do fish go on outings ?

By octobus !

★

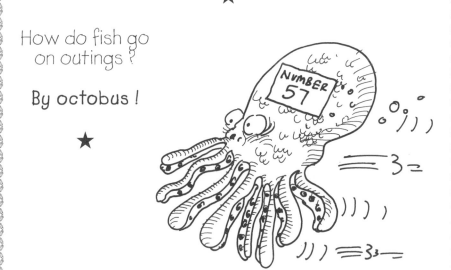

What sort of clothes do people wear
in very hot countries ?

Blazers !

Where are the Andes ?

On the ends of your armies !

Why do birds fly South in the Winter ?

It's too far to walk !

When bees go on vacation where do
they wait for the coach ?

At a buzz stop !

What has big ears, four legs, and a trunk ?

A mouse on a long trip !

Why did the elephant wear sunglasses on the beach ?

Because he didn't want to be recognized !

A witch wanted to go on a motorcycling trip...

...so she bought a brrooommm stick !

"Good morning ladies and gentlemen. Welcome aboard the World's first ever fully computerized aeroplane. There is no need for a pilot or co-pilot on this aircraft, as everything is fully automated. We are currently flying at 30,000 feet and everything is working perfectly...working porfectly...burking lurfectly...smirking carpetly..."

What type of crispy snack can you use to take you on a trip ?

Plane !

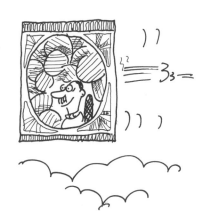

Where do bad cooks go to get away from it all ?

Greece !

Why do policemen like to go to
discos when they are on vacation ?

They really enjoy the beat !

What has big ears, a trunk, and flies you to
your destination ?

A jumbo jet !

*Three friends went on a cruise ship, but were
shipwrecked on a desert island. A good fairy
came and gave them one wish each. The first
two men wished they were back at home with
their families. The third man thought for a minute
and said, "It's quiet around here all on my own, I
wish my two friends were still here with me !"*

Did you hear about the elephant who couldn't
go on vacation - the notice said that all
cases, bags, and trunks had to go through the
airport X-Ray machine !

Waiter - do you have frog's legs ?

Yes, monsieur !

Well, hop into the kitchen and
get me a steak !

Why can't you play hide and seek
with mountains ?

Because they peak !

What's the shakiest vehicle in the skies ?

A jelly copter !

Did you remember to bring the
sun-protection cream ?!

**Yes, but I would have thought the sun
would be used to the heat by now !**

My annual outing was in ruins this year !

I'm sorry to hear that !

Oh! it's OK - I went on an
archaeological dig !

Why do monsters put people in their suitcases ?

They like to take a packed lunch !

Dear Santa..

I've been good - really means - **I haven't broken any windows for a whole week now !**

I'm kind to dumb animals - really means - **I sometimes help my little brother with his homework !**

I help old ladies to cross the road - really means - **I dropped a bottle of cooking oil outside the old folks' home and they all skidded on it !**

I stay behind at school all the time to do extra work - really means - **I am constantly in detention !**

I look forward to receiving a little something from you in my Christmas stocking - really means - **Fill up the huge garden sacks and three pillow cases with presents big man or there'll be trouble !!**

Where does a monster sleep when he
goes camping ?

In a sleeping bog !

What do people wear on their heads
in very cold countries ?

Ice caps !

Where do jockeys go on vacation ?

Horse - tria !

Where do carpet layers go on vacation ?

Floor - ida !

How do cavemen sit on planes ?

They fly club class !

Why did the cow use sun tan oil ?

Because she didn't want to tan her hide !

Why are you eating
all those baked
beans ?

I'm going windsurfing
this afternoon !

What has huge ears, four legs, and two trunks ?

An elephant going away for the weekend !

How do football players go on vacation ?

By coach !

How do fish go on vacation ?

By whale !

What do monsters like to eat best on vacation ?

Beaches and cream !

Where do you go to see the world's untidiest monster ?

Loch Mess !

Tourist - Can I have breakfast in bed ?

Hotelier - Of course, but most of our guests find a plate more sensible !

Mirthful Miscellany...

Did you hear about the girl who
fell asleep with her head
under the pillow...

...the Tooth Fairy came and
took out all her teeth !

Where has all the lemonade gone. I though we agreed to have half the bottle each ?

We did - my half was the bottom half, and I had to drink yours to get to it !

Cannibal 1 - I don't know what to make of my children these days ? !

Cannibal 2 - How about stew !

Doctor, doctor, my little boy has swallowed all the coins from my purse !

Don't worry - the change will probably do him good !

There were 10 cats in a boat, and then one jumped out. How many were left ?

None. They were all copycats !

Where does a vampire keep his money ?

In a bank a - Count !

What is made from fruit, served with ice cream, and moans all the time you're eating it ?

Apple grumble !

Where does a monster relax every weekend ?

On a ghoulf course !

What do you call a sheep with no legs ?

A cloud !

How do you make seven an even number ?

Simple – just take the "s" out !

Did you hear about the policeman who was invited to join the Royal Shakespeare Company...

...he always gave an arresting performance !

What did the scarf say to the hat ?

"You can hang around,
I'll just go on a head" !

What is the nickname of
London's tallest policeman ?

Big Ben !

What goes 'ho, ho, ho, ho, clonk'

Someone laughing their head off !

Why do witches fly around on broomsticks ?

Because vacuum cleaners don't have long
enough cords !

What did the policeman say to his tummy ?

I've got you under a vest !

What do you do if your nose goes on strike ?

Picket !

What tables can't you eat ?

Vegetables !

Why do bicycles never do anything exciting ?

Because they are always two tired !

What do you have to know before you can start training a pet ?

More than the pet !

What comes after the letter A ?

The rest of the alphabet !

How do you lift an elephant ?

Sit him on an acorn and wait for it to grow !

I would tell you the joke about the bed...

...but it hasn't been made up yet !

Why do elephants have such large ears ?

To act as ele-fans !

What does an elephant
do when it rains ?

Gets wet !

How do you stop your dog barking in the back of the car ?

Put it in the front !

What is worse than finding a maggot when you bite into an apple ?

Finding half of one !

What is brown and sticky ?

A stick !

What's the bounciest food at a Chinese restaurant ?

A spring roll !

What caught the wizard's drink when he knocked it over ?

His sorcerer !

How do you cut through the waves ?

With a sea-saw !

What sort of nuts
sneeze the most ?

Cashews !

What musical device
follows a bee ?

C D !

Why did the owl make
everyone laugh ?

Because he was
a hoot !

If your cat ate a lemon what would he become ?

A sourpuss !

Will you remember me tomorrow ?

Yes !

Will you remember me next week ?

Yes !

Will you remember me next month ?

Yes !

Will you remember me in a year ?

Yes !

Knock, knock

Who's there ?

You see, you've forgotten me already !

Knock Knock...
Who's there ?
Ivor...
Ivor who ?
Ivor good mind not to
tell you !

What four things contain milk ?

Butter, Cheese, er... a cow
and the truck from the dairy !

What did the man say when he went in to the
bank to arrange a mortgage and was served
by a masked man ?

I'd like to see the loan arranger, Lone Ranger !

How do you catch a vampire
fish ?

With bloodworms !

Why is a bee like the police ?

They both have a sting in
them !

Did you hear about the man
who was so stingy that the
moths in his wallet starved to death !

Did you hear about the cabbage whose friend won the lottery ?

...he was green with envy !

Yuck - this lettuce tastes of soap !

Of course it does, I've just washed it !

What happened to the man who discovered electricity ?

He got a nasty shock !

Why do witches keep pet cats ?

Because they like to see a familiar face around the house !

How do you make a fruit punch ?

Give it boxing lessons !

What did the
vampire with a cold
ask his doctor for ?

Something to stop
his coffin !

Cannibal 1
- Hello dear, I've
brought
a friend home
for dinner !

Cannibal 2 -
Why didn't you
tell me ? I've just
cooked a lasagne !

MMmmm! That cake was lovely and warm !

It should be - the cat has been
asleep on it all afternoon !

What's that crackling -
are you listening to an old radio set ?

No, I'm eating a pork sandwich !

How do you know when a bicycle is angry ?

It has a cross-bar !

Should you cycle to school
on an empty stomach ?

You could, but it would be easier on a bicycle !

What did the teacher ghost say to the
talkative pupil ghost ?

Don't spook until you're spooken to !

We went round the world on a big trip last year !

Where are you going this year ?

Oh, somewhere different !

I would tell you the *joke* about the highly contagious disease...

...but I'm sure you would get it straight away !

★

What is green and turns red at the flick of a switch ?

A frog in a blender !

★

Why was the vampire kicked out of school ?

He failed his end of term blood test !

★

Tarzan - Hello, operator, I want to speak to the King of the jungle !

Operator - Sorry, the lion is busy!

★

Jim - Does your watch tell the time ?

Joe - No. I have to look for myself !

Sailor - you have splinters in your hand !

Yes, I was leafing through the captain's log !

Why did the farmer send his cows to the gym twice a week ?

He wanted low fat milk !

Which insect breathes fire ?

A dragonfly !

Why do wizards have fond memories of school ?

Because they always came top in spelling !

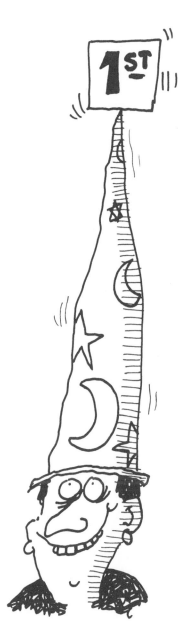

What do you call a vampire's leader ?

A Neckerchief !

What do you give a vampire for Christmas ?

Blood bath salts !

What do monsters do at the disco ?

Break dancing !

Where do you take a sick bird ?

To the casualty wing !

Why did the boy wave
his phone around ?

**Because he was told to
"hold please" !**

How can you help save a sick vampire ?

Stick your neck out for him !

What do you call a
vampire who likes
dipping biscuits
in his blood ?

Count Dunkula !

Why did the chewing gum cross
the road ?

**Because it was stuck to the
chicken's foot !**

Why couldn't the baker go to
the football game ?

He had no dough !

What can you give a sickly robot ?

Iron tablets !

Which part of a computer squeaks ?

The mouse !

What is the difference between someone in a hurry and someone wasteful ?

One makes haste the other makes waste !

What does a modern Santa Claus deliver presents in ?

A Holly - copter !

I wish I had been born 200 years ago !

Why is that ?

Because there wouldn't have been so much History to learn at school !

Sickly
smiles...

Do you know him - he's the hunchback
of Notre Dame ?

I don't know the name - but his face
rings a bell !

After the monster had bitten off both my legs
the police refused to arrest him !

Why was that ?

They said he had no arm in him !

What's green and hairy and has 18 legs ?

I don't know !

Neither do I, but it's just crawled up into your shorts !

Why did the chicken cross the road ?

I don't know !

It was going for an eye test, which explains
why it got hit by a bus !

What did the bus conductor say to the monster
with 3 heads, no arms, and 1 leg ?

Hello, hello, hello you look armless, hop on !

Doctor - Stand in front of the window and stick out your tongue.

Patient -Are you going to examine it ?

Doctor -No, I just don't like the man who lives in the house opposite !

What do you call a deer with its eyes poked out ?

No eye deer !

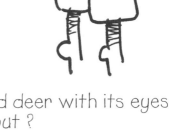

What do you call a dead deer with its eyes poked out ?

Still no eye deer !

Those chocolates were nice - but why were they furry ?

My brother sucked them up into the vacuum cleaner !

Why was the monster eating a horse in his bedroom at two in the morning ?

He was having a night mare !

Why did the fruit packer lose his job ?

He kept throwing away bent bananas !

What's the first thing a monster eats after he's had his teeth checked by the dentist ?

The dentist !

Where do you find monster snails ?

On the end of monsters' fingers !

Waiter - why is there a frog in my soup ?

To catch the flies !

Waiter, why have you got your thumb in my soup ?

I have a boil on my thumb and the doctor said I have to keep it warm !

What's the best thing to do with a green monster ?

Wait until he's ripe or you'll get tummy ache after eating him !

Did you hear about the really stupid woodworm ?

It was found dead in a housebrick !

What is green and white and swings through the trees ?

Tarzan's handkerchief !

What is black and white and red at the bottom ?

A baby zebra with diaper rash !

What climbs up and down bellropes and is wrapped in a plastic bag ?

The lunchpack of Notre Dame !

What is black, floats on water and swears ?

Crude oil !

A fat man went into the doctors and asked if the doctor had anything to keep his belly in...

...here's a wheelbarrow !

Jim - If there are ten flies on a table and I kill one with a newspaper, how many will be left ?

Joe - Only the dead one !

What vegetable do you never want to see in a boat ?

A leek !

What did one toilet say to the other toilet ?

You look a little flushed !

Did you hear about the man with two wooden legs who caught fire ?

He burned down to the ground !

What did one sick coffin say to the other sick coffin ?

"Is that you coughing" ?

Did you hear about the explorer
who escaped from the cannibals ?

It cost him an arm and a leg !

Doctor - You have four minutes left to live !

Patient - What am I going to do ?

**Doctor - You could boil
me an egg ?!**

What did the sick elevator say ?

"I think I'm coming down with something" !

A man was sitting in the park with his baby in
his lap and he was clearly very angry. A passer
by asked him what was wrong.
The man replied "I have just been insulted in
that shop over there. They said my baby was
the ugliest child they had ever seen!"

**"That's terrible," replied the passer by,
"tell you what, you go in there and give
them a piece of your mind, I'll hold
your monkey for you !"**

Did you hear about the man who
stole a truck load of prunes ?

He's been on the run for 6 months !

Dad, do apple pies have legs ?

No, of course not !

Oh! Then grandad has just eaten the tortoise !

Why did the jockey take a bale of hay to bed ?

To feed his night mares !

Why did the vampire have to go
and see his bank manager ?

**He had been spending too much on his
blood bank account !**

What do you call a scruffy, unreliable and
dishonest individual with no legs ?

A low down bum !

What is the difference between
a black cloud and someone who has just
had their toes run over ?

One pours with rain
the other roars with pain !

★

Waiter - why is there a dead mouse
in my soup ?

You would be dead too if you'd eaten
any of it !

★

Waiter, why are there ice cubes in my taco ?

Well, you said "extra chilly" !

★

Why should you always try to stay awake
when you are on a train ?

Because trains run over sleepers !

What did the doctor give the monster
for his liver ?

A sack of onions !

Why was the broom late ?

It over-swept !

How do you stop a skunk from smelling ?

Cut off its nose !

Doctor, doctor, I feel half dead !

**Well, I will arrange for you to be
buried from the waist down !**

How do you get a mummy interested in music ?

Play him some wrap !

What do you call...?

What do you call a Scottish
cloak room attendant ?

Willie Angus McCoatup !

What do you call a man with a calculator on his head ?

Adam !

What do call a place where aliens go to see films?

Cine- Mars !

Rodents always win gold medals in which sport ?

Ka-rat-e !

What do you call someone with a pair of shoes on their head ?

A sole singer !

What do call a man with 6 arms ?

Andy !

What do you call the young lady who lives in the coffin next to dracula's ?

The ghoul next door !

What do you call a man with a duck on his head ?

Quackers !

What do you call a small horse following someone ?

A Pony tail !

What do you call a frog who can leave his car anywhere ?

A Parking Kermit !

Where in the world do parrots come from ?

Polly-nesia !

What do you call a man who can sing and drink cola at the same time ?

A pop singer !

What do you call a cat that is always having accidents ?

A catastrophe !

What do you call a machine for counting cows ?

A cowculator !

How can you light a fire with one stick ?

Easy – if that stick is a match !

What sort of pet would a vampire own ?

A bloodhound !

What kind of dinner does an executioner look forward to ?

Chops !

What do you call the man who writes all Dracula's jokes ?

His crypt writer !

What did the doctor say to the fish with seaweed stuck on his head ?

He told him to seek kelp !

What do you call work that fairies have to do after school ?

Gnomework !

What do you call a streetlight where monsters hang around waiting for victims ?

A ghoulpost !

What do you call the carpet cleaner that vampires use ?

A victim cleaner !

What do you call it when your teacher is having a baby ?

A Miss-conception !

What do you call a screwdriver belonging to a toad ?

A toad's tool !

What do you call the place where cats have fashion shows ?

Catwalks !

What do you call a dead parrot ?

A Polygon !

What do you call a Tibetan chicken ?

Himalaya !

What do you call someone who doesn't use a hanky ?

Greensleeves !

What do you call a prisoner's pet parakeet ?

A jailbird !

What do you call it when someone tries to rob a bank with a bunch of flowers ?

Robbery with violets !

What do you call the largest mouse in the World ?

Hippopotamouse !

What do you call a boomerang that won't come back ?

A stick !

★

What drink do teddy bears like best ?

Ginger bear !

★

What do you call the skeleton who was once the Emperor of France ?

Napoleon Boney Parts !

★

What do you call a cat that works in a hospital ?

A first aid kit !

★

What do you call a cat that plays the drums ?

A drum kit !

What do you call a cat that makes models ?

A construction kit !

What do you call a snake that grabs a bowling ball ?

A bowler constrictor !

What do you call the last man to abandon ship ?

Deaf !

What do you call someone who drives all his customers away ?

A taxi driver !

What do you call the explorer who was caught and eaten by cannibals ?

Captain Cooked !

What do you call a cat that only knows 9 stories and bores people to death with them ?

A cat-o-nine-tails !

★

What do you call a machine for counting snakes ?

An adder-ing machine !

★

What do you get if you get hit on the head with a hatchet ?

A splitting headache !

What do you call someone who's been buried for 200 years ?

Peat !

What was the name of the man who invented Italian radio ?

Macaroni !

What do you call a vampire with a calculator on his head?

The Count !

★

What do you call the pliers you use in math ?

Multipliers !

What do you call the smelliest and hairiest royal person in the World ?

King Pong !

What do you call something with no legs that runs across the bathroom floor?

Water!

What do you call two banana peels?

Slippers!

What do you call it when a witch feels ill after flying?

Broom sick!

What do you call a cake you eat in the bath?

Sponge!

Most snakes have a university degree in which subject?

Hiss - tory!

What do you call out
when your toadstool
bag is almost full?

**There's not
mushroom in it now!**

What do you
call the lectures
about giblets that
monsters attend?

Organ recitals!

What do you call the writer of books
about very old furniture?

Anne Teak!

What is the result of smoking?

Coffin!

What do you call the skeleton of a snake?

A rattler!

225

What do you call the section of the army with the youngest soldiers ?

The infantry !

What do you call a robbery when you know you'll get away with it ?

A safe robbery !

What do you call a bicycle that snarls at people ?

A vicious cycle !

What do you call the instrument a skeleton plays ?

A trom - bone !

What do you call a candidate with a
parrot on his shoulder ?

A polly-tician !

What do you call a
Teddy that's been
buried in the garden ?

Plan - ted !

What do you call the flea on the moon ?

A Lunar - tic !

What do you call a cat that you
can rest your head on ?

Cat - a - pillow !

What do you call the secret file on a dog ?

Con - fido - dential !

What do you call the place where a
cat does his cooking?

The kit - chen!

Why was the snake charmer talking rubbish?

He always talks Cobras!

What do you call it when thousands of animals
rush to post letters?

Stamp - ede!

What do you call the cross
between a cat and a
butterfly?

Kiterpillar!

What do you call a man with
a washing machine on his
head?

Otto Matic!

How do you unload a ship full of snails ?

Open the escargot doors !

★

What do you call
spooky
schoolbooks ?

Exorcise books !

★

What do you call the food that horses eat
every day ?

Their stable diet !

★

What do you call a young dog
that eats flowers ?

A Poppy !

★

When do monsters eat fried eyeballs ?

On Fried - eyes !

What sort of creature ate my mother's sister ?

An aunt eater !

What do you call a flying dinosaur monster ?

Terror dactyl !

What do you call a fake noodle ?

An impasta !

What do you call a man with a toilet on his head ?

John !

(Of course he might have two if he was feeling flush!)

What do you call twin brothers, each with a drum on his head ?

Tom, Tom !

What do you call a cat in a panic ?

Cat flap !

What do you call the biggest ant in the World ?

An elephant !

What do you call a house where Martians live ?

A greenhouse !

What did the Martian say to the gas pump ?

**Take your finger out of your ear
when I'm talking to you !**

What do you call a dog that likes doing
experiments ?

A Lab-rador !

What do you call the stuff your milkman delivers
if you live at the end of a two mile cobbled
street ?

Yogurt !

What do you call the dance where all the rolls
are invited ?

Abundance !

What do you call it when two cows
munch grass side by side to keep warm ?

Double grazing !

What do you call a sheep dog when
it has eaten too much melon ?

Melancholy !

What do you call a highly dangerous cake ?

Atilla the bun !

What do you call the dessert that was served
after the battle of the Little Big Horn ?

Custer's slices !

What do you call a cake you can use to
power your portable CD ?

Current cake !

What do you call a cake you can give to mice ?

Cheesecake !

What do you call a cake you eat in the bath ?

Sponge !

What do you call a dog that likes wrapping presents ?

A boxer !

What do you call a madman who has a wash then runs away ?

Nut, washes and bolts !

What do you call the children of the Czar of Russia ?

Czar- dines !

What do you call a chimney built upside down ?

A well !

What do you call the most unhealthy bird ?

The Puffin !

Final Fling...

Whose daddy was a *mummy* ?

Tutankhamen !

Joe - Last night I opened the door in my PJs !

Jim - Why on earth have you got a door in your PJs ?

What do you call a bird drinking two drinks at once ?

Toucan !

Did you hear about the monster who ate a settee and two chairs for lunch ?

He had a three piece suite tooth !

Dad, can you help me with my homework, I'm trying to find the lowest common denominator ?

That's strange, they were trying to find that when I was at school !

Why did the fly fly ?

Because the spider spied her !

What do you get if you cross a pig with a dinosaur ?

Jurassic Pork !

When the monster had finished his supper he asked his mother if he could leave the table.

She said yes he could, as long as he had eaten the chairs!

Why did the carpenter fall asleep on the job ?

He was board !

Why did the spy stay in bed ?

He was undercover !

What do you call an environmentally friendly, noiseless, biodegradable food mixer that uses no electricity ?

A wooden spoon!

How do you stop a mouse from squeaking ?

Oil it !

Which two kings were good at fractions ?

Richard the third and Henry the eighth !

Who was the first man on the moon ?

A spaceman !

What lies under your bed at night with its tongue hanging out ?

Your shoe !

Waiter, why is this
chop so tough ?

It's a Karate
chop, sir !

KEEEAAA!!!

★

Joe -
Which is the best side to have
the handle of a teacup on?

Jim –
The outside !

★

I

would tell you the joke
about quicksand...

...but it might take a
while to sink in !

★

I wish you wouldn't cheat when we
play cards !

How do you know I'm cheating ?

Because you're not playing the hand
I dealt you !

What did the clock do after it ate ?

It went back for seconds !

What did the pencil say to the paper ?

I dot my "i"s on you !

Have you heard about the boy who kept
a pencil in his bedroom...

...so he could draw the curtains every morning !

Little Miss Muffet
sat on a tuffet,
eating a burger and rice.
A monster named Billy
ate Miss Muffet with chilli,
and said 'by golly that was nice !'

Teacher - Name three birds that can't fly.

Pupil - An ostrich and two dead sparrows !

What is a good parting gift ?

A comb !

★

What did the Pink Panther say when he
stood on an ant ?

Dead Ant, Dead Ant,
Dead Ant Dead Ant Dead Ant
Dead Ant Dead Ant...

★

How do ducks play tennis ?

They use a tennis quack-it !

★

Why was the baby goat a crazy
mixed up kid ?

Because he fell into the spin dryer !

Why was the cat lying on the toast rack ?

It was a marmalade cat !

What would happen to a penguin
in the desert ?

The chocolate would melt !

Have you heard about the boy who kept
a pencil in his bedroom...

**...so he could draw the curtains
every morning !**

*Little Miss Muffet
sat on a tuffet,
eating tandoori and rice.
A monster from Bury
ate Miss Muffet and curry,
and said 'by golly that was nice !'*

Teacher - Name three birds that can't fly.

Pupil - An ostrich and two dead sparrows !

Why did the cannibal go to the wedding ?

**Because he heard they were going
to toast the bride and groom !**

★

Hostess - does this aircraft travel
faster than the speed of sound ?

No Madam !

**Good, because my husband and I want
to talk !**

★

What does a music teacher take to the supermarket ?

A Chopin Lizst !

★

What did the tie say to the hat ?

You go on ahead and I'll hang around here !

Booklist...

The Complete Gardener

by

Rosa Cabbage

How to Combat Stiffness

by

Arthur Ritus

The Sandwich Makers' Book

by

Roland Butter

The Titanic Story

by

I.C. Water

Operator, can you put
me through to the zoo ?

Sorry, the lion is busy !

What can you tell me about
the Dead Sea ?

I didn't even
know it was sick !

How do you flatten a spook ?

Use a spirit level !

What do you call a homeless snail ?

A slug !

Little Miss Muffet
sat on a tuffet,
eating a piece of cheese.
Along came a mouse
the size of a house,
now little Miss Muffet's deceased !

Teacher - I wish you would pay
a little attention Blenkinsop !

Pupil - I'm paying as little as I can !

Why were you breaking the speed limit ?

I was trying to get home before my gas ran
out !

Where were all the Kings
and Queens of France
crowned ?

On the head !

What is the best time to pick apples ?

When the farmer is not at home !

Spell a hungry bee in
three letters !

M T B !

Why did the sprinter run across everyone
sitting in the park ?

Because his trainer told him to run over
twenty laps !

How do you make a cat happy ?

Send it to the Canary Isles !

What sort of pens do cry babies use ?

Bawl points

What does Dracula drive
when he visits relatives ?

A Vanpire !

Which runs faster, hot or cold water ?

Hot - because you can catch cold !

Why do oysters never share their food ?

Because they are shell fish !

What kind of underwear do reporters wear ?

News briefs !

When can you take jelly beans to school ?

On a chews day !

Why are teachers welcome in pool halls ?

Because they always bring their own chalk !

Where do teachers get all their information ?

From Fact - ories !

Why do doctors hate teachers when they come
to see them ?

Because they never give them enough
time to do the examination !

Knock Knock...
Who's there ?
Scot...
Scot who ?
Scot nothing to do with you !

Knock Knock...
Who's there ?
Cher...
Cher who ?
Cher this orange with me - it's too big for me
to eat on my own!

Knock Knock...
Who's there ?
Bob...
Bob who ?
Bob down and I'll pass your letters
through the catflap !

What boat can two cats sail ?

A catamaran !

What goes *moo, moo*, splash !?

A cow falling into the sea !

What do you get if you train a reindeer
to be a hairdresser ?

Styling Mousse !

My parents think you're great...really means...

...They think someone as weird as you
will put me off boys/girls for
the next 10 years !

★

What do monsters fasten their
suitcases to the car roof-rack with ?

Franken - twine !

★

Wow, it's hot in this stadium,
I'm boiling !

Well, come and stand next to me -
I'm a fan !

Why do monsters not mind being
eaten by kindly ghosts?

**Because they know they
will always be in good spirits!**

Who brings Christmas presents
to werewolves?

HO
HO
HO!

Santa Claws!

Where did the cook learn to make banana splits?

In sundae school?

Well, Mr. Blenkinsop, your cough sounds much better this morning !

So it should, doctor, I've been up all night trying to get it right !

★

Doctor, doctor, I think I'm a dog !

Well, take a seat and I'll have a look at you !

I can't - I'm not allowed on the furniture !

Doctor, doctor, my wife thinks
I'm a hypochondriac !

Why haven't you been to see me before about
this ?

I've been too ill !

★

Doctor, doctor, I think
I will have to
give up jogging !

Why ?

**Because whenever I
stop my nose
keeps running !**

★

What do you get if you cross a
frog and a cold drink ?

Croaka - cola !

★

Who serves the meals on a spooky
plane ?

The Air Ghostess !

What do you call a German barber ?

Herr Dresser !

Did you hear about the man who went
to the doctor and told him he
thought he was a piano ?

The doctor gave him a note !

What do you call a wobbly book full
of telephone numbers ?

A jellyphone directory !

What sort of fast food
do aliens like best ?

Nuclear Fission Chips !

What sort of sea creature flies a spaceship ?

A Pilot Whale !

Have you heard about the
inter-galactic magicians club -

- called the flying sorcerers !

Our coach once tried to swim
across the English channel !

Did he do it ?

**No - he got halfway across and had to
turn back because he was so tired !**